EMERGENCY EXIT

RECENT POEMS BY XHEVDET BAJRAJ

Translations from Albanian and Spanish
By Ani Gjika and Alice Whitmore

Egret
CHAPEL HILL
2020

First Edition

Printed in the United States of America

Cover and book design by Maxine Mills
Cover photograph by Francisco Trejo

Laertes

Egret is an imprint of Laertes Press, Incorporated | www.laertesbooks.org

YOU HAVE FORGOTTEN

You have forgotten
what the river is
what the flower is
what the sun and the sky
you have forgotten
what the word is
what the outstretched hand and
what the gleam in the eye are
you have forgotten lips
what lips mean
to other lips

—AW

SHADOW

This world is a beautiful shirt
but it doesn't fit my body
he told himself
and he extinguished the bedroom light
took a knife and fork
and began to eat the darkness

When the sun surfaced
he had turned into shadow
only the knife and fork
were left alive

—*AW*

TAKE REVENGE

Come

let's warm ourselves like magpies

on the rooftops of those abandoned houses

wounded

by mortars in the last war

Under the gap-toothed smile of the sun

let's lie naked

and warm ourselves

Because we are poor

and love is the only weapon we have

with which to take revenge on life

—AW

THE LAKE

The lake was surrounded by a forest
he and she were making love
among the oak trees
like children
back when all civilization was a child
It was a sunny day
a pair of nightingales sang on the branch of one oak
some children swam in the deep lake
they were happy
On top of a hill a feral dog
that for ten years since the war has been waiting for its owner
to come out with his family from the bottom of the lake
It had seen them being dumped there
but not being executed

—*AG*

FOOTNOTE

When they buried the first man
a terribly beautiful animal was born
at the lip of his grave
it drank sadness from the teat
of the bitch of life

Later on
the beast began to write
poetry
in the footnotes of death

—AW

WAKE UP

She naked with a cup of coffee in one hand
walks to the window with a chair in the other
she looks to the street where the dogs
nose for food among the garbage
before the trucks come and take it away
(she has fallen asleep in the chair)

I am naked lying on the bed
with a cup of coffee in one hand
and in the other a lit cigarette
I try to stop time
before the clouds hoodwink the sun
and send her to work for twelve hours a day
until the day she retires
and force me to tend to these flowers that bloom in loneliness

Still, freedoms are violated in broad daylight

between the extinguished eyes of the ones who voted

and the insatiable eyes of the ones they elected

Wake up

Life has an expiration date

time waits for no one

—AW

AS FAR AS POSSIBLE

In countries
where youth is the only good
exported on the global market
no one takes care of the elderly
whereas the hungry consume this idiocy
as if it were whiskey

People need to move away
as far as possible
far
even farther
where there's no need for sleeping pills
or bombs
or bullets
or knives

—*AG*

THE POLITICIAN

He falls asleep exhausted
awakes exhausted
goes to work exhausted
lives his exhausted life

Have mercy
turn off the TV
so the politician can rest

—*AG*

THE PEDDLER OF SMALL WOODEN ANGELS

As it does every blessed day
the night has laid a golden egg and escaped
this time clucking lightning

It wakes the fire inside the stone
wakes the birds
the sleeping babies wake
the mothers wake with the milk in their breasts
the morning flowers wake
and the drowsing loves
and the dead who dwell in memory
the sunflower seed merchants
the paralyzed
the train and bus drivers wake
the good people with jobs wake
and so do
their killers

Every day they wake

        clenching life between their teeth

he too

the peddler of small wooden angels

wakes

with a feeling of embarrassment, because he is a man

but he wakes in vain

Carrying his full bag from house to house

every blessed day

but not a single person opens the door

—*AW*

EMERGENCY EXIT

Every house
every landscape
every homeland in a dictatorship
must have
an emergency exit
kept free 24 hours a day
in case we need to escape
even if just for a moment
some hours
or forever
from the dark image of life

And to return obviously
to light a candle near that image

—*AG*

THE APOCALYPSE RIDING ON A WHITE HORSE

During the war

there were many victims in the cities

where people hauled water

to boil two eggs

To accomplish this

men lit fires at first with old newspapers

then comics

magazines

Marx's books

Engels's

children's literature

followed by chapters

of history

philosophy

short story collections

novels

religious scripts

they learned their favorite poem by heart

and then burnt that page too

or wiped their asses with it

Later the enemies retreated

people celebrated their freedom

and prepared to welcome

the Apocalypse riding on a white horse

at least this happened in Kosovo and Bosnia

now it's happening in Syria Iraq Libya and Afghanistan

—*AG*

IF THERE HAD BEEN LAMBS

The roses had just begun to emerge from their shells
the sun was gliding across the blue ice
and
if there had been lambs in Kosovo or in Mexico
they would have been running through the green fields

A mother cat gave birth to four dead cubs
she lay bleeding in the street

The afternoon sky grew furious
it began to snow
and nobody could recall
a time when it had snowed so heavily
onto the heads of the newborn roses
and the lambs that did not exist

The mother cat stood up in her own blood
and pushed out three more stillborn kittens
then she died

—*AW*

THE LESSON

People need to learn from scratch
what war is
what peace is
They need to learn to walk
carrying a heart full of love
on the palm of their hand
open under a sky
full of predatory birds
People need to learn from scratch
to spread sunlight
or a storm on a piece of bread
and share that with their neighbors

—AG

LITTLE RED RIDING HOOD

You can't convince me
that on a winter's night returning home
we've never walked on snow
with your hand in my pocket
that you weren't wearing a red hood
and your boots weren't red, too
It's not at all possible that we didn't kiss
that we didn't warm each other's lips
with our souls' heat
It can't at all be possible
that we didn't find a warm place
a candle
a bottle of red wine
and we didn't make love

Or does it mean that I long for
that which I once dreamt of?

I am a wolf
but it doesn't matter
if the lamb obscures my brandy
or that my days are ending
waiting for little red riding hood
at the crossroads of life's blind track

—AG

FAIRY

I see her often in dreams
naked in the middle of the woods
dancing with the beams of moonlight
before the astonished eyes of a wolf
and for a moment
life is better

She does not know
that I have put her in my poem

—*AW*

THE MUSE AND THE POET

At the dawn of humankind

those times when darkness still ruled the world

on top of a mountain in the middle of a forest

a man and a woman

in the dark

were speaking heart to heart.

They were both naked

when the man touched the woman between her legs

a voice from the sky was heard saying

let there be light

and there was light

and poetry was delivered

—AG

INSTRUCTIONS ON HOW TO WRITE POETRY

Art plays with the unknown
marks its territory like a wild animal
uses the sun
walks across your shadow
and when you know the time
you will understand that the mind can be manipulated
but the heart cannot

Uproot the heart
speak to it in the language of graves
squeeze it in your hands
what spills out
is poetry

—AW

IN SILENCE

I

A broken man chain-smokes his cigarettes

in silence

in the black limbs of the night

in silence

the fruits of loneliness ripen

in silence

freedom (paid for in blood)

clothed proudly in corruption

walks

in silence

through blind streets

II

A butterfly dies against the window in silence

a plant blooms against the same window in silence

life agonizes in silence

the sun reemerges in silence

the man refuses to wake

in silence

—*AW*

THE SUITCASE

From the refugee's suitcase

one can never

unpack

what made it here from his birthplace

—*AG*

THE CRYING VINES[1]

Their footsteps disappeared
along the paths of the homeland
just as the snow was melting
and the thorns were emerging in the atriums
where the vines weep
from the houses of old abandoned men
with burning lips and mouths
souls burning
with the heat of their
always boiling memories
pointlessly they blow on their spoons

How easily dreams arise there
how easy it is to lose the path that takes us to them
when the vines are crying

---

1. Each year, before the vine leaves emerge, they cry honey.

Everyone will understand once
how difficult life is in Kosovo
how easy it is to die there

One time
everyone will understand
how long
and how pained the heart cries
how pained the vines cry
before healing over

—AW

THE YEAR THAT BROUGHT NO SPRING

The light cast by the sun of sadness
dries the tears
of a swallow
who has nowhere to return to
This time the year
brought no spring

—AW

TABLEAU OF WAR

Nothing moved inside the frame
fires from each chimney all put out
the trees slept birdless
from the breast of a murdered woman
ran milk
as if wanting to quench for good the thirst
of the man looking at the painting

—AG

THE OTHER ROAD OF RETURN

A child with a spoon hanging on his neck
exits a fairy tale and enters our reality
and with that spoon eats very little life, in a hurry
and in a hurry returns to the fairy tale
before the murderer has a chance to invent
a new road to return home
a new landscape
where the child would have slipped
on his own spilled blood

—*AG*

HOME SWEET HOME

The storks returned to their nests some time ago
the river carries dead fish on its back
decapitated hens run lifeless
the young men drinking in the cantinas of the city
since the early morning
dream of a better future
their executioners smile from television screens

Dear reader
I'm asking in earnest
doesn't this place look familiar

—AW

LIFE FLOWER

The moment he sets foot on the soil of Arizona
a young man is surprised by a bullet
that makes its nest in his head
a cactus flowers in the desert
crossing that desolate landscape an angel in Huichol dress
rides a blue stag
in and out of two parallel worlds

The echo of a train whistle
that hasn't passed this way in half a century
is like a greeting to the echo of the image of a woman
standing on the veranda of her house
she returns the greeting with the movement of a handkerchief

The Horse With No Name is still running across the prairies
in search of a more anonymous name

An old man in the middle of Mexico City
has been praying for five hours
to the worm at the bottom of his mescal bottle
and finally he convinces it to be eaten
now the old man can rest in his bed
he won't hear the too loud voices of his memories
crying out
with one click he switches off the tv
with another click he switches off himself

Through the open window and mixing with the moonlight
the perfume of a flower of shit
all is quiet

—AW

THE DANCE

Someone killed the night

peeled it

and with its skin covered the city

people didn't feel cold anymore

a young man was looking for his lover

but had forgotten

that just two hours ago they'd plucked out his eyes

he tried to touch her

but touched death

He took off his shoes

and slipped inside a coffin bought at a discount

began to dance with his lover

for eternity

—*AG*

AGONY

Now it snows slowly

a bad snow

small and cold

When I see through the window

those abominable snowflakes

that the storm throws to and fro

I feel a desperate

yearning

for you

It's the feeling

    of a man in his death throes

        who agonizes

and holds out his arms

and claws at the air with his nails to survive

Even more than that

let's say I am clawing at the sky

so that I might

hang from your neck

and kiss you

—*AW*

THE NOISE

Sidewalks are filled with people

stores

restaurants

wrapped in noise

the sun scorches

From the kidnapped child

under anesthesia

they remove a kidney

After some hours

they bury her with dolls

so she won't be upset in heaven

—AG

A DROP OF WATER

A poet's life
a drop of water
that refuses to flow down to the sea
vaporizes
and returns to the earth
to feed a plant perhaps
or to quench a butterfly's thirst
just when it chucks its caterpillar garb
on the new grave
Someone needs to teach angels
how to descend to earth

—AG

A BALCONY LOOKING ONTO THE SEA

I don't know if love is still keeping her alive
I am going to her now
I am flying over the ocean

I imagine her naked in the library of her house
painting something in the air
a house with a balcony looking onto the sea
a house with a desk
two chairs
two cups of coffee
a bottle of brandy
an ash tray
and a flock of birds flying over the sea

—*AW*

THE BATTLE OF LOVE

A she-wolf
the moment of insemination
lets out a howl
shatters the black winter sky

A man
gives up his dreaming
leaves the bed and his warm room
naked
runs to the forest

Two hours later
snow covers the tracks
of the battle of love
and they say
there are no survivors

It was all a marvelous misfortune

—AG

ON THE RIVERBANK

The sun is born
wild animals drink from the river
butterflies sail overhead
        they do not alight on the riverbank
the birds are singing
an angel descends from the sky
holding an empty sack

On the riverbank a willow weeps
Bobbing now to the surface of the water
the toes, nothing more
of a dead man
and the tip of his nose

—*AW*

FORGIVENESS

Looking at a pair of birds
building a nest
I am reminded how
when you're a child
your mother bathes you
combs your hair
clothes you
feeds you
tucks you in bed
tells you stories
When you're older
you are stunned to see yourself
naked in a wild environment
among beasts and you run to put on clothes
to cover yourself
you hide
dress in camouflage

then attack

but you can never

learn the skills of the beasts

because your mother told you from the crib

that you are human

So you forgive her

for having lied

—*AG*

The following poems were taken from the volume, *The Year That Brought No Spring*, published in 2018:

You Have Forgotten

Take Revenge

The Lake

Footnote

Wake Up

The Peddler of
Small Wooden Angels

The Apocalypse Riding
on a White Horse

If There Had Been Lambs

In Silence

The Year that
Brought No Spring

The Other Road of Return

Home Sweet Home

Life Flower

The Dance

The Noise

A Drop of Water

A Balcony Looking
onto the Sea

On the Riverbank

The following poems were taken from the volume, *When the Vines Weep*, published in 2019:

Shadow

As Far as Possible

The Politician

Emergency Exit

The Lesson

Little Red Riding Hood

Fairy

The Muse and the Poet

Instructions on
How to Write Poetry

The Suitcase

The Crying Vines

Tableau of War

Agony

The Battle of Love

Forgiveness